Lake Superior Rock Picker's Guide

Lake Superior
Rock Picker's Guide

Kevin Gauthier
and
Bruce Mueller

The University of Michigan Press
Ann Arbor

Petoskey Publishing Company
Traverse City

Copyright © Kevin Gauthier and Bruce Mueller 2007

All rights reserved

Published in the United States of America by

The University of Michigan Press

and

The Petoskey Publishing Company

Manufactured in the United States of America

⊛ Printed on acid-free paper

2011 2010 2009 2008   5 4 3 2

ISBN-10: 0-472-03267-4   (paper: alk. paper)

ISBN-13: 978-0-472-03267-9   (paper: alk. paper)

Library of Congress Cataloging-in-Publication Data on File

Acknowledgments

To my Camper-dos,
I am looking forward to many more rock hunting trips with you!

—Kevin J. Gauthier

This book is dedicated to my wife, Shirley, who has done
my typing and checked spelling and punctuation for all
that I have written for the last fifty years; to my son Kevin,
who did the computer work on my last two books; to my son
Paul who has walked many times with me ten miles or more
along the lake shore; and to the tens of thousands of
geologists working for hundreds of years whose distilled
knowledge of the earth has been passed down to all of us.

—Bruce E. Mueller

Contents

8   *Lake Superior Rock Picker's Guide*

Color photographs *following page 64*

Introduction

This book was written to answer questions on Lake Superior similar to those we answered for Lake Michigan beach stones in our book, *The Lake Michigan Rock Picker's Guide* (ISBN 978-0-472-03150-4).

What kind of stone is this?
Where is it from?
How did it get here?
How was it created?
Where can I best find that special stone?
If it's copper, how can I clean it?

Rocks and minerals are best described not by words, but by color pictures. This book and its pictures should be a useful guide for anyone wishing to explore and more, importantly, understand the Lake Superior shoreline and the copper, iron, and gold mines near its shores.

Collecting

Rules for collecting along park shorelines vary. There are Canadian provincial parks, U.S. national parks, state parks, county parks, township parks and city parks. Rules sometimes change, so be sure to inquire before collecting. In general, the larger and the higher the park's designation is, the less likely it is that collecting will be allowed. With smaller parks where no one is on hand to ask, there may be signs saying what is and is not allowed.

Outside the parks, there is usually no realistic way to know who owns a piece of land; it may be private property, state property, or federal property. It is best to inquire locally. Rock shop owners and rock club members, contacted through a local chamber of commerce, will be glad to help. Dial 411, say what city and state you want and ask for the number of the chamber of commerce. Even some of the small towns will have a chamber of commerce. Rocks and minerals, along with fishing and hunting, and the beauty of the area are what bring people into the Lake Superior region. People in the region are eager to help, and on pages 99-101 there is a list of people who are knowledgeable and willing to be of assistance.

The region around the lake is of such obvious mining potential that Native Americans began mining here 5 to 7 thousand years ago. On the Keweenaw Peninsula and Isle Royale, they mined hundreds of millions of pounds of copper by hand. Their mines guided more recent miners to many of the more important copper deposits. Iron ore was discovered in 1844. Iron, copper, gold, and silver have been mined here for many decades.

If you obtain permission to collect on private property, you are then responsible morally, if not legally, to remember that you are collecting at your own risk, not at the property owner's risk. If you sue the property owner, you may be able to collect, but if you do, all of us will look around one day and see no trespassing signs in every direction as far as the eye can see, and rock collecting will be a thing of the past. Be careful; use good judgment. A teacher, without asking permission, drove a bus load of children on a working day into a quarry where collecting had been allowed. Explosive charges had been set all around the rim of the quarry and were about to be detonated. The school bus doors opened. The children scattered all over the quarry. No one ever collected there again.

Remember, whether you are along the lake, in a park, or on private property, get permission, follow the rules, use good judgment, be careful, and stay safe. Happy hunting.

For listing of parks see the following web sites:

www.wisconsondnr.com
www.dnr.state.mn.us
www.parks.state.mi.us
www.Canadaonline.about.com

Lake Superior's Rocks

The surface area of Lake Superior is larger than that of any lake on earth. Once around its shore would be a journey of 2725 miles. On route you would find rocks of nearly every color, kind, description, origin, composition, and age. To the north of the lake lie two million square miles of Canadian Shield, the ancient core around which North America grew. The Wisconsin Glacier, active from about 70,000 years ago until about 7,000 years ago, driven by sunlight on the Northern Hemisphere, wrapped its icy fingers around every rock it could find to the north and transported them south. Some of the rocks along Lake Superior's shores may have come from the Arctic coast of Canada. Some came from the floor of Hudson Bay. Some came from the floor of Lake Superior, said to be the most highly mineralized place on earth. Some came from areas now covered by Canadian forests and from the floors of, what are now, Canadian lakes.

The glacier brought us rocks and minerals from places we could never reach and left them within an easy day's drive of the Midwest and its largest cities: Minneapolis, Milwaukee,

Chicago, Detroit, Cincinnati and others. Roughly 50 percent of the rock on the lakeshore is of glacial origin. The rest is bedrock or pieces of bedrock broken by waves. If you know what the bedrock will be, you will know in advance much of what is to be found on any beach. Most of what the glacier brought is predictable. The remainder is nature's grab bag. While on these beaches you have 2725 miles of beach rock to explore–washed clean, rounded and nearly polished by 2500 years of wave action.

Many people come to these beaches to look just for Lake Superior agates. They are the oldest agates known. Because of physical and chemical circumstances peculiar to that time and place, these agates can be readily distinguished from all others. Lake Superior agates of unusual size and quality may be priced at $5000 and up. Agates are only one of hundreds of different treasures the lake has to offer.

Lake Superior is itself a treasure. Its water is clean, clear, and blue-green; no algae, no zebra mussels. The shoreline is rugged and in places, it is semi-mountainous. Just offshore many islands beckon. In the entire Lake Superior basin there are just over 600,000 people, nearly all of them crowded into 5 major cities. Here, unlike elsewhere, you will not find access to the beach blocked by shoulder-to-shoulder homes, resorts and the usual commercial clutter. This is an accessible lake of great beauty.

While on these beaches, don't just look for agates or for whichever rock you came here to find. Broaden your field of view. Learn to see everything here; and beyond that try to see what was here when these stones were being created.

The earth, quite by accident, has written its own autobiography. Each stone is part of that autobiography with its own story to tell. The earth that existed when some of these stones formed had an atmosphere of methane and ammonia without oxygen. The land was barren; no plants, no animals. The early moon was closer, its gravitational attraction 100 times what it is today. Today's 5 foot tide would, in those early days, have been a 500 foot tide. The moon, as it rose above the horizon 100 times its present size in appearance, would have been a sight for which the word awesome is inadequate. With the moon so close, asteroids more abundant in earlier times blasted rubble from its surface into space. With the earth that close, some debris landed on earth. Somewhere in those old rocks, perhaps in pudding stone, perhaps in the Gowganda tillite, there are stones from the moon, but we do not yet know which stones they are. Somewhere buried with those old rocks there is evidence of early tides, volcanoes, lava floes, mountain ranges and events about which we know nothing.

Walk ten paces on any Lake Superior gravel beach and you will find something totally bizarre, unexpected and delightful, if you allow yourself to see and understand what's really there.

Lake Origins

The coast lines of Africa and South America, separated by the Atlantic Ocean, appear to fit together like two pieces of a gigantic picture puzzle. This led Wagner and others to suspect that the continents are adrift; not on a sea of lava or magma, but rather on a sea of rock hot enough to be lava were it not under enormous pressure from overlying rock. The continents, like icebergs, drift on slow currents of underlying hot, but not molten rock. They drift across the face of the earth, sometimes colliding, sometimes separating. They drift at about the rate your fingernail grows. The Atlantic Ocean, which separates the old and new worlds is a product of 190 million years of drift. Had you and a friend been standing on opposite sides of the rift that separated these worlds, each never cutting one of your fingernails for the last 190 million years, your fingernails would today just touch above the mid-Atlantic rift, the fracture that has separated the old and new worlds.

At times, due to the vagaries of earth's convection currents, controlled by forces we do not and may never understand, continents collide and assemble to form super continents. Twice, so far as we know, all continents have been brought together as super continents, and twice these super continents have been torn apart and scattered across the face of the earth.

One billion one hundred nine million years ago what was at that time the North American Continent began to split along a rift that follows the gentle arc of the basin in which Lake Superior lies. That portion of the crust was on its way to becoming an ocean basin. The rift valleys of East Africa, filled with lakes and active volcanoes, exemplify what the Lake Superior landscape would have looked like. As the split widened, over a period of 25 million years, hot basaltic lava floes spread from open fractures in the crust and associated volcanoes. Look anywhere on today's lakeshore and you will find black basalt from those days. Other volcanoes erupted rhyolite, the volcanic equivalent of granite, and rhyolite also is to be seen everywhere. Toward the center of the rift, volcanic debris accumulated to form a layer nearly 12 miles thick. Volcanic activity in the rift ended when the breakup was stopped by a collision between North America and another continental land mass. About 20 million years after volcanism stopped, hot water solutions from below, perhaps originating in the monumental pile of lava floes that lie below the lake, perhaps from somewhere deeper, brought copper and other minerals toward the surface. The 12 billion pounds of copper mined from the Keweenaw Peninsula is only a hint at the mineral wealth that lies on the floor of Lake Superior. Later the rift filled with sedimentary rock, especially with sandstone, as seen along the lake's southern shore. Very recently, beginning only about 70 thousand years ago, the Wisconsin Glacier removed this soft sediment to create the lake basin, as we know it today.

Bedrock around the Lake

The northern shore of the lake is a patchwork quilt of igneous rock; some of it extrusive, some intrusive. The extrusive rock consists of volcanic ash and lava floes. The intrusive rock cooled below the surface slowly, producing rock with large crystals such as granite and gabbro.

The southern shore is, for the most part, sandstone from Pre-Cambrian and Cambrian times. The four exceptional areas are all on the Keweenaw Peninsula or its approaches. These areas are marked on the Lake Superior map as areas 1, 2, 3 and 4. These areas are, in turn, enlarged on the following pages.

On these maps the letters represent:

SS   Sandstone

K   Kona dolomite

VS   Volcanic and sedimentary

M   Michigamme slate and included graphite

PLV Porter Lake volcanics

CHC Copper Harbor conglomerate

NIF Negaunee iron formation

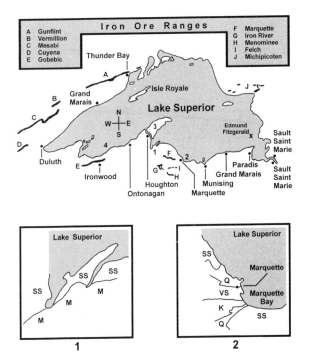

Iron ore range data from *Geology of Michigan* by Dorr and Eschmann. Courtesy of the University of Michigan Press.

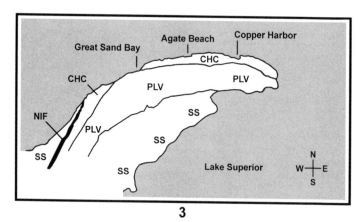

3

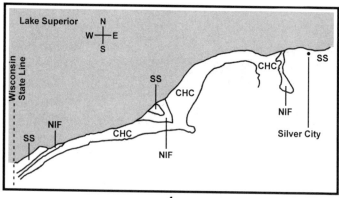

4

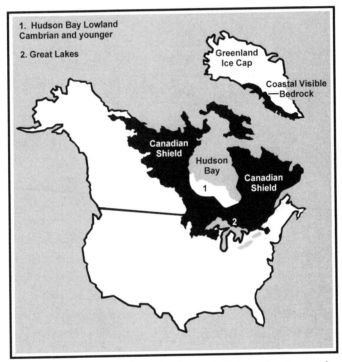

Canadian Shield data from *Geology of Michigan* by Dorr and Eschmann. Courtesy of the University of Michigan Press.

A Trip around Lake Superior

Since the trip around Lake Superior is like driving from New York to L.A. (through two different countries) we will break up the collecting around this massive lake into two separate trips. The first will stay on the states side, starting at Sault Ste. Marie, Michigan, across the Upper Peninsula of Michigan, through Wisconsin into Duluth, Minnesota, and then north to the Canadian border. The second will start from Sault Ste. Marie, Canada, north to Wawa then west to Thunder Bay, Canada, ending on the United States side.

Where the bedrock is sandstone, as is true of most of the southern lake shore, you will be collecting from glacial drift and from stones driven east along the lake shore by waves driven by wind from the west. Waves hit the beach from the west, roll up the beach at an angle, and then move back down the beach under the influence of gravity. Wave by wave, year after year, and century after century, pebbles on the beach drift east along the shore. The sandstones themselves are responsible for a series of spectacular waterfalls; Tahquamenon, Laughing Whitefish, Lower Au Train and others. They are also responsible for the spectacular cliffs at Pictured Rocks near Munising, Michigan. A good map is useful; the better the map, the more useful it is. I recommend the *DeLorme Atlas and Gazetteer of Michigan* ISBN 0-89933-335-4 available at almost any book store. On this map you will see where eastward moving sand grains, released by wave action against the sandstone pictured rocks, have rounded a point at AuSable Light House and encountered a sheltered area behind the point, where they are stored in the Grand Sable Dunes, dunes of awesome size, largely due to earlier water levels. The dunes rise 200 feet above the lake's surface.

Should you visit the log slide on these dunes (well worth seeing), you will see signs warning that if you slide down the dune here and are not killed on the way down, which is probable, you will get down in 30 seconds. But it will take 3 hours to get back up. The log slide is a section of dune, down which early lumbermen slid logs into the lake.

A Trip around Lake Superior—United States

Sault Ste. Marie, MI to Whitefish Point, MI

At Bay Mills, east of Sault Ste. Marie, the bedrock is sandstone. Nevertheless, there is good collecting here from glacial drift pebbles and cobbles, as well as from the eastward drifting wave-driven pebbles. Here and to the east is your best chance, on this lake, to find pudding stone, whose source is to the north and east. Pudding stone, as well as other collectible rocks and minerals, are listed alphabetically and discussed on later pages. The further west you go, the less pudding stone you will find. Associated with the pudding stone is Gowganda tillite from the same source. There are several types of hematite here, probably from the Michipioten Iron Ore Range. There are jaspers, Lake Superior agates and thompsonites brought from the north by the glacier and driven from the west by the waves. Good ones are not common, but I have seen an agate from this area that is more than seven inches in diameter.

At Point Iroquois Light, west of Bay Mills, you will find the same types of pebbles and cobbles lining the shore and the lake floor as those seen at Bay Mills. Here, as well as at Bay Mills, you will find an attractive, dark-colored stone filled with pinkish-yellow inclusions. It is probably a metamorphosed andesite porphyry.

From Iroquois Light to Pendills Creek, nearly anywhere you stop, there will be stony beaches and a stony offshore lake floor. These stones are similar to those at Bay Mills and Iroquois Light. To the west and north to Whitefish Point the bedrock is sandstone with little glacial gravel.

Whitefish Point is unique, powerful northern storms have blown unobstructed across nearly 350 miles of water. The lake funnels waves into a narrower and narrower space, concentrating the energy stored by gale force winds in three quadrillion gallons of water, down to what is, virtually, a point. Waves split the *Edmond Fitzgerald*, a 729 foot long ore carrier, in half and sent it to the bottom so quickly that its radio operator, talking on the radio at the time, just suddenly stopped talking. Whitefish Point is a finger of land pointing out into the lake to the east, the direction in which the waves travel. Sand, gravel and stone are driven down the beach and out into the lake at the point. With every storm, the point grows a little more. On a good map you will see Marsh Lake, Little Lake and others that curve in such a way as to show where the point once was before it grew to its present size. If you would like to see what real waves can do to stone, come to Whitefish Point. Stones here have been pounded repeatedly, one against another, until they are the most rounded stones you are ever likely to see anywhere. At Whitefish Point you will find basalt, granite, jasper, gneiss, hematite, metamorphosed andesite porphyry, and an occasional Lake Superior agate. If you want round stones, this is the place to come. At the lighthouse there is a museum, well worth seeing, with memorabilia from many of the ships that have gone down nearby.

Two Hearted River, MI to Marquette, MI

West of Whitefish Point is Crisp Point Light. Here, and at the mouth of the Two Hearted River, there is the usual amazing assortment of glacial drift, including unikite and Lake Superior agates. Rivers, such as the Two Hearted River, which bring gravel from inland are good places to find material newly brought to the beach.

Further west is Sucker River at Grand Marais. Grand Marais is French for big marsh. Don't worry, the marsh is to the southeast, and quite a marsh it is. There is an extensive gravel deposit here, extending both to the east and west. The most common rock here is a streaky gneiss, from north of Wawa in Canada. (On page 38 you will see a picture of a road side outcrop.) Enough Lake Superior agates have been found here to warrant establishment of a museum, the Gitche Gumee Agate and History Museum. For information regarding hours and collecting contact Karen Brays (906) 494-2590. The road to the east along the lake leads to good collecting beaches, but you will need a Jeep to get there. Karen's book, *Understanding and Finding Agates* is ISBN 0-9760559-0-2.

Just west of Grand Marais are the Grand Sable Dunes and the Pictured Rocks.

West of Munising, at Christmas, turn right at the state furnace sign, just across from the gas station, to see a nearly intact charcoal smelter. The beach is littered with slag. Slag is not a mineral, but comes close to being one and is of interest. Slag is covered in the alphabetical list of minerals. It is a glass which is the by-product of smelting iron ore.

Near Marquette, as shown on map enlargement 1, are four types of beach bedrock, other than sandstone. Two of the layers are quartzite. Quartzite is metamorphosed sandstone, in which individual sand grains sometimes glimmer in response to light, as in the well-known green aventurine from India. Some quartzite is locally collected and cut and polished. This is the Goodrich quartzite. Sandwiched between the two beach zones, underlain by quartzite, is a series of rock layers called the Chocolay

Group and another series of volcanic and sedimentary rocks. The Chocolay Group has two members of considerable interest. One is the Fern Creek tillite, which seems to be the same age as pudding stone. It is metamorphosed glacial debris, like pudding stone, but less spectacular, with a more random assortment of pebbles. The other member is the Kona dolomite, known to nearly everyone who has ever cut and polished stone. These two layers date to about two billion four hundred million years ago, with the Kona being the younger of the two. Here, looking for Kona on the beach, you will be in downtown Marquette. A better place to look is at the Lindberg Quarry, near town, where Kona can be purchased at a nominal price. Directions to the quarry are listed in the alphabetical mineral list under dolomite.

The volcanic and sedimentary group can be seen (the Marquette granite) along the river near Dead River Bridge in Marquette. The granite here contains green epidote crystals.

Keweenaw Peninsula, MI

On map enlargement 2 the bedrock, at the southern tips of Huron Bay, and at L'Anse, at the southern tip of Keweenaw Bay, is slate. Slate is not very interesting, but this slate contains lenses of graphite. Graphite is not very interesting either, but this graphite is from floating mats of vegetation; the first vegetation known to have been abundant enough to produce graphite and also coal, as found at Iron Mountain, Michigan. Near L'Anse, where U.S. 41 begins to pull away from the bay going east, stop and walk east along Pebble Beach. Another place to look, perhaps better, is on Route 41, south of L'Anse 7 miles. On the DeLorme map you will see two crossed shovels representing an old quarry near the road where graphite was mined. Inquire locally. The slate is perhaps two billion years old.

The Copper Harbor conglomerate near Copper Harbor, MI

On map enlargement 3, the Keweenaw Peninsula, there are two principal types of bedrock; the Portage Lake volcanics and the Copper Harbor conglomerate. These layers range in age between one billion one hundred nine million years and one billion years old. Basaltic lava floes and other volcanic debris reached a thickness, near the center of the lake, of about 12 miles and spread out about 100 miles to the north and south. Volcanism here lasted for about 25 million years. Gas bubbles in the lava preserved as cavities were connected by fractures resulting from cooling, enabling ground water to bring in minerals in solution to create agates, thompsonites and a host of other minerals. These lavas and others to the north are the source of Lake Superior agates and many other minerals found everywhere along the lake. Weathering and erosion of these lavas produced the Copper Harbor conglomerate.

Twenty million years after volcanism stopped, hot water moving upward through these lavas brought in copper and other minerals. There are well over 100 collectible minerals here.

In map enlargement 4 the only new layer of bedrock is the Negaunee iron formation which furnishes hematite, iron ore, jasper, chert and flint along with many other minerals. This formation also reaches the lake as a narrow band shown on map enlargement 3.

Saxon, WI to Duluth, MN

Further west at Saxon Harbor, walking west, the shore-line consists of a high clay bank, probably representing mud deposited in the lake during a glacial retreat and then pushed back out and onto shore by a glacial advance. This clay contains what are locally called Lake Superior concretions. Elsewhere they are called loess kin-chions (children of the loess). We found several in a short walk on the beach. These clays and concretions continue on into the Bad Axe Indian Reservation. Do not enter the reservation without permission.

The Bayfield Peninsula and Apostle Islands are under-lain by sandstone resulting in a generally sandy shore line, but agate, hematite, and jasper from the north shore in Minnesota are present here, as well as other minerals.

Rounding the corner of the lake at Duluth you will be on the Canadian Shield. The Canadian Shield actually begins with the western half of the Upper Peninsula of Michigan, but here in Minnesota the shield becomes very apparent. The coast line here is a patchwork quilt of lava floes, ash beds and coarse grained igneous intrusive rock. Route 61 hugs the lake, passing through two tunnels cut through gabbro, an intrusive slow cooled form of basalt. Along this shore to the Canadian border it is possible to find agates and thompsonites almost anywhere, but they are not common. A good book listing the many beaches that are open to hunting is the *Rock Pickers Guide to Lake Superior's North Shore,* ISBN 0-967379-30-X.

Lake Superior agates at Two Harbors, MI

At Two Harbors a rock shop called Agate City has an excellent display of agates from nearby beaches. At Gooseberry Falls State Park, near a little town called Castle Danger, it is possible to find agates and pieces of crystalline calcite in white rhomboid shapes on the beach. Trails leading north out of the park and west from near the park lead to rivers where agates may be present in places where streams have gravel bottoms. Those who fish Minnesota's streams north of the lake report finding many agates while fishing.

Split Rock Lighthouse, MN to Canada's Border

At Split Rock Lighthouse to the northeast, the lighthouse sits atop a massive cliff composed of anorthosite, an intrusive igneous rock, which is believed to have floated upward to the surface in a sea of molton basalt.

Split Rock Lighthouse on top of a cliff of anorthosite

At Beaver Bay, the Beaver Bay Agate Shop has an excellent display of locally found agates. Just east out of town across the bridge is a place to park and walk down to the river. Because of the stream, there is much gravel here. In addition to agates, you will find pieces of chert. This is not just any chert; it is gunflint chert from the Gunflint Iron Range to the north. It ranges in color from black to white

with green, brown, red and maroon in between. Found in
the gunflint chert in the 1950s were what were, at that
time, the earliest known well-preserved fossils. They were
two billion one hundred million years old. These were
bacteria-like organisms capable of photosynthesis and
were probably responsible for the iron ore deposits. They
can be seen in thin sections of chert under a microscope,
but there is no guarantee that every thin section will
contain fossils. Larger and more complex, but similar
organisms, were found in the Negaunee iron formation,
some in strands several feet long. At Grand Marais running through town is the Gunflint Trail, the old trail
followed by those early pioneers who needed flint to spark
the firing of their guns. Along this trail, flint (chert) was
collected by early hunters and trappers. The trail is now
Route 12.

To the northeast, along highway 61 from Grand
Marais about 13 miles, near milepost 123 is Paradise
Beach. Here opaque agates are found with white and red-
dish-orange banding that is unique. A very nice beach.

From Portage near the Canadian border, it is possible to
take a ferry to Isle Royale. In Canada at Thunder Bay it is also
possible to get a ferry to Isle Royale, and from the Keweenaw
Peninsula a ferry to Isle Royale is available: Some boats do
not run on windy days. It is best to check first.

A Trip around Lake Superior—Canada

Lake Superior's north shore will remain the Great Lakes last frontier for rock collecting until personal hovercrafts come into production. The terrain makes it very difficult to access the lakeshore. There is no convenient winding road that dips in and out of the shoreline with scattered parks and pull outs near the water's edge. Most of the north shore is a very rugged terrain with one road (#17) running through mountains of granite. Many times on Canada's #17 you are separated from Lake Superior by 300 foot sheer drop offs and miles of very rugged terrain before the shoreline is reached. This leaves hundreds of miles of shoreline virtually untouched. One can only look over the majestic lookouts and wonder what treasures are resting on the shoreline just out of reach.

Lake Superior's shoreline makes it almost impossible to land on the stony beaches by boat. Even an experienced captain would not go to shore with large protruding rocks and sheer cliffs with waves smashing up against them. Even on a calm day, mariners know that Lake Superior can change in an instant. This leaves some of the best treasures yet to be discovered. On the North Shores, I have seen areas where the smooth rounded rocks are piled 20 feet wide and a foot and a half thick. These can run for hundreds of miles without a single road leading to them. Agates, copper nuggets, silver nuggets, and a host of other gems will be picked up from these remote places by our great, great grandchildren from their newly manufactured personal hovercrafts. Until that day comes, many miles of shoreline will be walked with a lot of sore feet and backs looking for that perfect gem stone.

Canada's Ontario License Plate reads "Yours to discover."

Miles of untouched shorelines and islands below this ledge near Lake Helen, Canada

More miles of untouched shoreline in the distance

Entering into and Returning between
United States and Canada

As you are crossing the international bridge, you will want to have your passport and the birth certificates for your children. You will be asked if you have any firearms, alcohol, or tobacco, where you are going and how long will you be in Canada. Upon your return, you are asked how long were you in Canada and where are you returning from, and did you bring anything back with you? When I asked the Canadian border patrol about bringing rocks back from Canada, he indicated that there is a U.S. and Canada agreement that states no Aggregate may go between borders. This law is intended to keep the soils that collect on the stones from crossing borders. He then added that if I had a few pocket rocks for souvenirs and they were soil free, I probably would not be bothered. We both left it at that.

Sault Ste. Marie, ONT to WaWa, Batchawana Bay, and Agawa Bay

Immediately as you enter Canada, you will see the visitor's center. At the visitor's center there are clean restrooms, you can exchange money, and there are many, many maps and brochures to pick up. The visitor's center is very helpful with information. I would advise you to make a stop here. About an hour across the border on highway 17 north towards WaWa you will find Batchawana Bay Provincial Park, which has lots of camping facilities. As you continue north around Montreal River you will begin to see huge outcrops of unikite (pinkish-red granite with streaks of green epidote) where the road was cut through. These outcrops of unikite run for 10 to 15 miles up into Lake Superior Provincial Park. Here the unikite is some of the finest in the world. The streaks of green have a very intense contrast with the red background. The streaks of epidote create some very unusual patterns in the rocks. From Lake Superior Provincial Park back to Sault Ste. Marie, Michigan, many pieces of beautiful unikite can be found on the shoreline.

Lake Superior Provincial Park (www.lakesuperiorpark.ca) is 130 km (a 90 minute drive) northwest of Sault Ste. Marie, Ontario, and the northern boundary is only 15 km (a 10 minute drive) south of WaWa, Ontario. It offers a vast number of attractions for outdoor enthusiasts. Canada's provincial parks are similar to United States national parks in regards to collecting rocks. Provincial Parks Act 952 states *"Except with the written permission of the Minister [of Natural Resources], no person shall remove any relic, artifact, or natural object."*

There is no collecting of rocks in the park; however, the scenery is beautiful and the shoreline is majestic. Agawa Bay Campground offers campsites right on Lake Superior, but on a windy day you may want to camp a few sites inland. If you are not a camper, the Ontario parks also offer day-use permits. Throughout Agawa Bay you will see many types of granite—black and white, reds, some pink, but primarily you will find the gray-to-black and white types. A lot of stones observed here are streaky gneiss (striped black and white rocks). This is not surprising since you will see outcrop after outcrop of this type of granite as you drive north on 17 through the park. However, the most interesting rock was the abundance of unikite seen throughout the bay.

Agawa Bay Campground, looking north down the shoreline

An outcrop of streaky gneiss   A similar outcrop at the beachfront would break down to stripped beach rocks

Of interest in the park for the rock enthusiast are the Agawa Rock pictographs (rock paintings). "The trail is short, but very rocky and rugged. The trail passes through some interesting geological features: rock chasms, broken boulders and sheer cliffs. This is a sacred site where generations of Ojibwa came to record their dreams and spirits in red ochre. Caution is advised when venturing onto this rock ledge due to its slope and the unpredictable nature of Lake Superior and its wave action." www.lakesuperiorprovincialpark.com

A little more than half way though the park you will come to Gargantua Road on the left (west side) which will also lead you down to Gargantua Harbour. This road is rough so if you do take it to the shoreline, plan 30-40 minutes each way. This is not much of a harbor, but seeing the cove is overwhelming. There are hundreds

Looking north in Gargantua Harbour

of thousands of baseball-to-boulder size rocks on the beach as far as the eye can see.

A five-kilometer (or more) hike south along this shore line will lead you to Rhyolite Cove. Time and gear did not allow me to make the hike; however, I talked to some hikers who were coming back from this overlook and they said the trail was rugged. In this bay one can see scattered pieces of rhyolite, basalt, striped granite and quartz nodules. The bay is scattered with pieces of rhyolite. North of here, is an island called Devil's Wharehouse Island. A sailor showed me hand-size pieces of pink prehnite that came from this island. The prehnite must be restricted to the island as there was no prehnite, that I could discover, on the shoreline. After enjoying the rest of the views through the park, just outside the park to the north, is a great place to collect rocks. There is a roadside park on the left-hand side. It is right on the south side of Michipicoten River. A few hundred foot walk along a very shallow stony river will bring you to Lake Superior. Again, here you will find beautiful streaky gneiss, and with any luck, you may find an agate or two. Another sailor friend in our local rock and mineral club has found many beautiful agates on Michipicoten Island. Because of the prevailing winds and ice flow, material found on the shoreline of Michipicoten Island may also be found near the mouth of Michipicoten River.

Just north, WaWa offers several restaurants, overnight accommodations, gas stations, and the closest hospital since Sault Ste. Marie. This is a very historic place to visit and the visitor's center (you can't miss the large goose) offers you an awesome view and a lot of mining history. Just past the visitor's center, there is a little outside hamburger stand on the right side of the road (next to the trading post) with fantastic homemade hamburgers!

Some of the worlds oldest rock can be found in the mountains surrounding Michipicoten and WaWa. The mountains contain a melting pot of minerals that have attracted people since the 1800's. The Ojibway mined special veins of hematite to produce the bright red paints needed to produce their pictographs. In 1897 a trapper uncovered a rich vein of gold quartz. This brought a large influx of gold prospectors to the area. By 1900 the rich iron hills in the area were being transformed by Francis Hector Clergue into Helen Iron in WaWa, the Algoma Steel Corporation in Sault Ste. Marie, Algoma Central Streamline & Railroad companies.

The mucking machine, retrieved from the Kosak Mine (1930), has a 48-inch tall boy on the machine. In dark, cold, cramped conditions, a six-foot, 220 pound man on this machine would have had a long ten-hour day.

Mucking machine use in mining tunnels

WaWa's visitor's center, with the large goose monument, was built
to commemorate the opening of the last link in the Trans-Canada
Highway on September 17, 1960

White River, ONT, Marathon to Terrace Bay

Several different people have told me (some say just west, some say 20 miles west) about diamonds being found in the trout streams near WaWa. I have heard there have even been kimberlitic pipes found! If you are an angler and like diamonds this might be a good place to do some fishing!

From WaWa to White River is a little over an hour's drive. The road is cut though the granite knobs of the Canadian Shield. One begins to appreciate the immense amount of work and equipment it took to transform the solid granite knobs into driveable roads. (If you drive west of Terrace Bay, you will see some miraculous roads cut through solid granite mountains.) The rock that was dynamited away to create these roads can produce some very interesting pieces as well, especially the striped granites. In some areas, the road is being widened for passing lanes. The blasting of new granite produces fresh material to look at. Although tempting, I caution you not to just pull off anywhere. Find a designated area to park as the roadsides are narrow. This is the main trucking route across the north shore of Lake Superior. Forty thousand pounds of logs do not stop easily, and hospitals are few and far between.

Winnie the Pooh's hometown is White River. The World-famous children's character, Winnie the Pooh was inspired by an orphaned bear cub. She was purchased from a trapper in White River by Captain Harry Colebourn, during WW I. He was a veterinarian and stopped in White River enroute from his hometown of Winnipeg. He took her on to England as his troops' mascot. Hence the name "Winnie." The captain left her at the London Zoo where she was discovered by author A.A. Milne's son Christopher. Winnie inspired Milne to write the children's stories for his son. There is an annual festival held at the park. In the visitor's center, along with other Winnie the Pooh facts, you can learn about an enormous fire that almost consumed White River. The charred trees and new growth of vegetation can be viewed west of the city for tens of miles.

White River, Winnie the Pooh's hometown

As you continue west beyond White River there are several large mining operations that can be viewed from the road. These operations included platinum, gold, and silver mining. If you enjoy gold panning, this may be a good area for prospecting streams and rivers. Further west, 614 leads north to the town of Manitouwage. Here is home of the deepest silver mining operation— over 1 mile deep! So, yes, there are a lot of precious metals in this vast area. One needs to just locate a small vein near the surface to hit the mother lode!

Marathon is just beyond Pic River as you continue west. I am sure there is a lot to discover here, but we did not venture to the lakefront town. Instead we stopped at Terrace Bay just beyond Neys Provincial Park. The beach access provides an excellent view of Slate Island which seems to float in the endless expanse of open water. From Terrace Bay to Marquette, Michigan is the longest stretch (250 miles) of open water on all the great lakes. Terrace Bay, on this northern point of Lake Superior, is unique in that the sun rises out of vast stretches of open water and dips back into Lake Superior at the end of the day. The beach is a combination of yellow coarse-grained sand and gravel, making rock picking enjoyable in bare feet. Most of the picking here will be coarse and fine-grain granites, white quartz and feldspar; all remnants of the Canadian Shield.

Road cut west of Terrace Bay

West of Terrace Bay, the road (Canada's 17) is cut through rugged mountains making one feel insignificant as you pass through these cuts. Notice the size of the car compared to the road cut. A dear friend who used to make an annual trip pulling a 5th wheel told me these were 40-70 hills. When I ask what that meant, he smiled and said, "You drive 40 mph going up the hill and 70 mph going down the other side."

Rainbow Falls Provincial Park is west of Terrace Bay beyond Schrelibe. This stop is well worth the time. *"Cascading waters plunge over the rock ledges of Rainbow Falls on their way to Lake Superior. Trails, including the Casque-Isles section of the Voyageur Trail, lead to panoramic views. Choose to camp near the beaches of Whitesand Lake or along the rugged shore of Lake Superior at the Rossport Campground."* *www.ontarioparks.com*

Rossport, Nipigon, Dorion to Nipigon Bay and Black Bay

Beyond Terrace Bay are two picnic areas near Rossport, both are on the left-hand (south) side of the road. The second has a park on Lake Superior with picnic tables, grills, and outhouse accommodations. This beach is unique in that it has large, weathered, granite outcrops that dip into the lake, as well as a cove of smaller round rocks and a sandy beach. Again, you will primarily find granite, white quartz, feldspar, and granite with quartz and red jasper intrusions (striped rocks). Because you are able to walk safely on these granite outcrops, I highly recommend this little park area as a stopping point.

Weathered granite dipping into Lake Superior near Rossport

Beyond Rossport there are several rivers with gravel bottoms. Depending on the time of year and the winter run-off, you will have some great rock picking at the Cypress and Jackpine rivers. These two rivers are not named on a traditional road map. The Cypress River is between Rossport and Nipigon. The shoulder of the road is narrow, making it a little more difficult to pull off, so be careful. We stopped at the Jackpine River, which has a very large right hand turnout just after you cross the river (west side). This spot is easy to identify if you are traveling west. As you are coming down a large hill, you will see a massive "gravel" pit 50+ stories high and a bridge crossing near the bottom. The bridge has a green sign marked "Jackpine River." From the east, the river is not marked and it comes up quickly, but is 17.3 miles east of Nipigon. This glacial "gravel pit" is formed by a bend in the river eating away an old gravel moraine. The river's flowing action is continuously exposing new material. Rocks from one inch to boulder size are constantly rolling down the hill, so I caution you to be alert and <u>do not attempt to climb</u> this hill as it will create an avalanche of rocks. All the rocks previously mentioned can be found here with the addition of a red-and-white-colored sandstone. You will see outcrops of red and white layered rock along the road all the way to Red Rock, which is south of Nipigon.

Rock hunting at Jackpine River—rock hunting made easy.
The rocks roll down to you!

Picture of an outcrop near Red Rock, showing how the white and
red sandstone layers are compressed together. These are layers of
sandy sediment laid down on a pre-Cambrian sea floor.

Near the shores of Nipigon, about where the land juts out into Lake Superior, I was told by locals of a large basalt outcrop filled with Lake Superior agates. One could only reach this location by boat. Here drums of Lake Superior agate were extracted by blasting the basalt with dynamite, loosening the agates. One can only wonder how far into the bottom of the lake this basalt layer extends. How many agates have been weathered out of the basalt over thousands of years and are just off shore in deeper water?

As you emerge from the mountainous terrain, west of Nipigon past the Sturgeon River, the first farmland and hayfields are quite a surprise to see. It's as if they jump out from nowhere. The land becomes flatter leaving awesome views of Lake Superior in the rearview mirror. One can, however, look forward to two side trips; Ouimet Canyon Provincial Park and amethyst country!

Near Dorion is Ouimet Canyon. This canyon is a sheer-walled canyon that drops so deeply that it shelters rare arctic-alpine plants on the floor below. There are two viewing platforms with some remarkable views. Bring a camera. Blending into the surrounding nature is a network of boardwalks and trails. As one approaches this spectacular gorge you can feel the cool air rising from the depths below. At this latitude, with the canyon running east–west, very little to no sunlight ever reaches the canyon floor. I was told that snow can be on the canyon floor almost year round!

Beyond Dorion is amethyst country. There are several open mining operations that allow the general public to come in and dig through their expended rubble. There are signs along the highway for the different mining operations. If you are lucky, you will come up with a few nice points and small clusters. Most places will charge by the bucket or by the pound. Some more "touristy" spots will charge a cover charge just to get into the gift shop instead of charging by the pound to dig.

If you really want a prize piece you will have to get down and dirty with some hard rock mining. This type of digging is usually planned as a group fieldtrip through your local rock club. If this kind of digging is not in your plans, you can buy amethyst from the mines' gift shops or from many places selling amethyst along the highway. However, be aware that if the amethyst has a blue agate seam near its edge, a green exterior (host rock), and in a nice complete cavity (geode), it is probably a Brazilian amethyst and not the local amethyst. The local amethyst will usually have pink granite as the host rock. Canadian amethyst forms in the fissures of granite, and it is very rare, if ever, to extract a round geode. Brazilian amethyst forms in gas bubbles and almost always has a concave shape.

For some very nice amethyst at reasonable prices, I recommend stopping at Mirror Lake Campground and Gift Store. The owners of the campground have information on who has been working their mines (blasting fresh material) and the quality of material that is being found. They also know many of the private mine owners and have contact with them, allowing for a more diverse selection of amethyst. If you are planning to stay at the campground, call ahead for reservations, as the campground can fill up on the weekends.

Amethyst Country

Mirror Lake Resort & Campground is located 66 km west of Nipigon and 35 km east of Thunder Bay. This recreational campground has numerous nature trails and crisp, clear spring-fed lakes making for great fishing, canoeing, and swimming. For reservations call 807-977-2840.

Extracting amethyst at the Blue Point Mine

The picture to the left shows amethyst miners packing a dynamite charge into a hole drilled previously. Notice the amethyst vein is to the right of the miners.

The bottom picture is the same view after the dynamite charge has been set off. Notice how the precision of the blast only loosens rock to the left side of the vein and did not destroy the amethyst.

Studying where to hit the vein of amethyst   Making that critical hit
to best protect the crystal while removing
it from the solid granite

SILVER ISLET 1868

Off this shore lies Silver Islet, once a barren rock, measuring about eighty feet in diameter, where silver was discovered in 1868 by Thomas Macfarlane. The claim was purchased in 1870 by a company headed by A.H. Sibley, and one of the partners, W.B. Frue, was appointed mine captain. Frue waged a constant battle against the lake which undermined extensive crib work used to bolster the restricted working space. Despite this problem and the difficulty of housing miners and transporting supplies in the isolated region, this famous mine produced $3,250,000 worth of silver ore before it was closed in 1884.

Erected by the Ontario Archaeological and Historic Sites Board.

South of Pass Lake is Sleeping Giant Provincial Park where the
famous Silver Islet Mine produced $3,250,000 worth of silver before
it closed in 1884

Silver Islet. *Photos courtesy of Ed Rothgarber*

Beyond Pass Lake is Thunder Bay. The shoreline is heavily populated with mostly waterfront private land. Thunder Bay is the second largest city in Ontario with a population just over 100,000. There is a lot to do here with a lot of shopping and history. A short drive from Thunder Bay will bring you back into Minnesota.

The far north shore of Lake Superior is enjoyed best without the black flies and mosquitoes. Keep in mind the black flies are out mid-June through mid-August.

Beach Renewal

It is widely believed that big storm waves bring new stone out of the lake and onto the shore, but waves must touch bottom to move stones forward. It's easy to see where waves touch bottom; stand on the shore and watch. Offshore you will see a place where waves begin to slow down, bunch together, and increase in height. When waves touch bottom, the base of the wave slows more than the top. The wave pitches forward and "breaks." It is where the waves touch bottom, break, and cascade down onto the lake floor that waves can transform their energy into forward motion for moving stones. From this point to the highest point the wave can reach on the beach, wave energy can be transformed into stone motion. The larger the wave, the further offshore it can break. Big waves, where they break, pack an incredible punch. Thomas Stevenson, the father of Robert Lewis Stevenson, was the first to measure wave force. He measured their force on the Scotish seacoast at up to six thousand pounds per square foot. There is a recorded instance of a new concrete pier weighing 2,600 tons being carried away by storm waves at sea.

Why Are the Rocks on Lake Superior So Round?

Over a billion pounds of rocks are in constant motion on Lake Superior's shores—talk about alternative renewable energy!

Everyone loves a smooth round rock. Since virtually every rock on Lake Superior is round and smooth, the lake is a rock hunter's dream. Many people come to Lake Superior just to collect rocks because of their shape. You will find more round ping-pong-ball-sized rocks on Lake Superior than on any other lake in the world. Lake Gitche Gumee is the deepest of the Great Lakes. The pounding wave action continuously works on the stones. However, the wave action will make a rock close to round, but never reach perfect symmetry. At its peak of almost becoming perfectly round, it will take a new direction and the shape will become flatter and flatter, moving farther away from a perfect round symmetry. The best time to intervene is at this peak, saving it from future wave action. Ah, now you have a nice round rock for your collection.

One "calm" day, I sat and watched in a six-foot swath of Lake Superior's shoreline. Thirty gallons of rocks (420 lbs) were being tossed ten feet up onto the beach then dragged back ten feet through the coarse sand and then finally disappearing into the lake. This action repeated itself over and over and over. After watching this multiple times, I began timing the waves and came up with an average of 22 waves per minute. This meant that these rocks were tumbling through sand 633,600 feet per day! That's 19 million feet in one month. Now, add a windy day, with a storm or two, and that figure will increase dramatically! Lake Superior has 14,388,000 feet of shore line (2,725 miles). Every 2.7 seconds a little over a billion pounds of rock have moved 22 feet up and down Lake Superior's shoreline making it, by far, the world's largest lake-driven rock tumbler!

Arggh!! The large piece of mountainside shown here demonstrates the eminent force the wave action has in rounding even the largest boulders!

I have been told, by those who live along Lake Superior shores, that the largest storm waves they have seen are eight feet high. Others have said fifteen feet high. The *Andrea Dorea* is believed to have been sunk by waves 35 feet high, near Whitefish Point; not normal for Whitefish Point, and certainly not normal for the rest of the lake.

Those who live along the lake will tell you that waves, even big storm waves, break one to two hundred feet off-shore. The lake level has stood where it is today for the last two thousand five hundred years. Anything in that strip one to two hundred or even five hundred feet wide that could be moved, onto shore or to a point just offshore, has been moved already. Most of the lake is over 325 feet deep. Its average depth is 489 feet. Waves, not even *Andrea Dorea* waves, do not break at anything near such depths. What storm waves do is to turn over the beach stones that are already on shore. What was toward the bottom of a gravel beach sometimes ends up on top, and what was on top may end up toward the bottom. What storm waves can do, you can do to a lesser extent. Move some of the surface gravel with your foot to see what's underneath. A bulldoz-er would be even nicer, but I have heard that the food in jail leaves something to be desired. Much of the gravel on beaches is brought down to the lake by streams. There will be an unusual amount of gravel on the beaches where streams are carrying gravel rather than just sand. A good flood can bring in an incredible amount of new gravel. In fact, a good flood can double the depth of a river by moving gravel on the bottom in rivers like the Mississippi. Places where streams enter lakes are good places to look for rocks, especially after a heavy flood. Ice that freezes to the lake bottom can pluck loose new gravel unattainable by wave action alone. Shoreline erosion drops glacial gravels onto the shore where there are soft glacial deposits or soft bedrock that can be eroded. Yes, storm waves do bring new stones onshore from a strip just offshore, but not commonly and not many.

Common Stones

Common stones, were they rare, might be of some value, but because they are common they are of little value. It is worth knowing a little about them, however, because you will see them everywhere along the lake.

Sandstone is made up of sand grains which are, for the most part, fragments of weathered granite. The Canadian Shield to the north is mostly granite. The result of weathering of that granite is a layer of sandstone along the southern shore over 2000 feet thick. As sand travels with the wind, in streams, with currents, or just washes back and forth on the beach, the harder quartz grains grind against the softer feldspar grains reducing them to powder. The purest, whitest, quartz sandstones have traveled the farthest.

Granite, made up of feldspar and quartz, has a salt and pepper look. It represents magma that cooled miles below the present surface of the Canadian Shield, now exposed at the surface by prolonged erosion. Brought from the north by the glacier, it is found everywhere along the lakeshore. It is the youngest of the Canadian Shield rocks at perhaps two or more billion years old.

Rhyolite would have been granite had it cooled below the surface, but it was erupted from a volcano. It has large crystals slowly grown underground (phenocrysts), encased in fine crystals due to rapid cooling at the surface. These volcanoes, because their lavas are not very fluid, build tall, steep, straight-sided cones. Such cones once stood along the center of what is now Lake Superior. They are lost from our view, but not from our imagination. It is unlikely that any of the Lake Superior volcanoes attained the size of the older volcanoes that line the rim of the Pacific Ocean.

Andesite is more fluid than rhyolite. It builds tall steep cones, but because its lavas spread well beyond the summit, these volcanoes spread over a wider area, resulting in volcanoes with concave slopes. Like Mt. Fujiyama in Japan, they are everyone's idea of what a volcano should be. Andesite, at a glance, looks like basalt, but it is not as black. Some is very prophyritic with large crystals in a dark ground mass of fine crystals. These porphyries are often of great beauty. The large crystals are usually feldspar; some are iridescent, some may have a play of color or a moonstone effect. Volcanoes, such as these, once sat just offshore in the basin where the lake is today. There are many types of porphyry along the lake.

Basalt is very fluid, sometimes spreading quietly from

open fractures; sometimes producing low dome-shaped volcanoes known by the descriptive term shield cones. If you stood on the edge of such a floe or volcano looking upslope, you would see only an endless expanse of very black rock extending as far as the eye could see. Where the surface of a floe has cooled and crinkled during floe the resulting ropy textured floe is called pahoehoe. Some whose surface has broken up into rubble is called ahah because, it has always been suspected, that's what the Hawaiian islanders who crossed the stuff in their bare feet said. Both forms of lava can be seen today on the Keweenaw Peninsula and on the north shore. The granites of the shield are younger than the basalts of the shield. The basalts of the shield are younger than the gneisses of the shield and the volcanic rocks from the Lake Superior basin are younger than the rocks of the Canadian Shield.

Gneiss is a metamorphic rock changed, from almost anything, by the pressure that builds mountain ranges when coastal plates collide. It resembles granite, but its light and dark minerals are segregated into bands or streaks. It is from the Canadian Shield and is the oldest of the rocks to be found along the lake. Some are 3.6 billion years old.

Minerals

Many of the highly sought minerals found along the lake can be said to be amygdaloidal. Lava is driven out of the ground by gas pressure much like a soft drink will spray out of a bottle when shaken. Steam from heated ground water dissolved in lava is the most common gas. The upper surfaces of lava floes, where pressure is not great, are full of gas bubbles which remain as cavities in the lava once it cools. Hairline fractures, caused by the cooling of lava, connect these cavities to one another and to the surface. When ground water fills these cavities with dissolved minerals they solidify to fill the cavity with one mineral or another and the rock is said to be amygdaloidal.

The chemistry of volcanic ash allows silicon and other minerals to dissolve easily. Volcanic ash is finely divided, resulting in a huge surface area where solution can take place. Heated water from lava floes, which can stay hot for decades or from the subsurface, will dissolve minerals far more readily than cold water. In short, a lava floe is fertile ground for the solution and redeposition of minerals in the cavities (vesicles) that occur in lavas. The result: Lake Superior agates, thompsonites, chlorastrolites, and a nearly endless list of other minerals. Marquette County alone is listed as having more than 175 different minerals.

Agates

Lake Superior agates are amygdaloidal. They consist of relatively pure quartz deposited in gas pockets within lava. One cavity, if there was a way for water to enter, equals

Varieties

Lake Superior agates

Lake Superior classic red and white agates

Amethyst crystal, is still dirty as dug from a mine.

Amythest crystal, has the clay cleaned off of it.

Beach amethyst and amethyst in Lake Superior agate

Andesite, porphyritic

Basalt will be plain brown to
gray in color

Basalt, amydaloidal will have gas
bubbles that filled with other minerals

Probably metamorphosed
basalt porphyry

Ophitic basalt will look like Chinese writing on the stone

Binghamite will look like fibrous flames in quartz

Calcite will be creamy white, many times found with copper

Chert is usually found with gray and cream colored bands

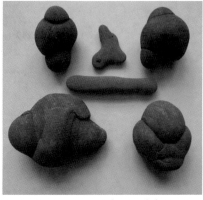

Concrections clay nodules

Lake-washed copper. Note where it has been touched with sand paper to expose the copper

Copper found in the mine dumps

Datolite bottom pieces are beach-washed

Diamonds, three at bottom of the dime

Feldspar dry will reflect light

Kona dolomite

Fulgurites are petrified lighting strikes

Garnets are often burgundy to red
in color

Goethite will be heavy and look irony

sand

gold dust

Gold will be malleable and scratch like
copper, unlike fools gold which will
crumble when crushed

Gowganda tillite

Granite will look like flakes of minerals
cemented together

Greenstone, left, from mine dumps;
on the right found on the beach

Greenstone beach pebbles. Note the
thompsonite mix in the lower right

Silver combined with copper from
mine dumps

Silver and copper, note silver right
of quarter

Hematite, botriodal will look and be
heavy like iron but have a bubble
texture

Specular hematite, top, large crystals;
bottom, small crystals

Jasper usually red in color

Sliced jaspelite

Jaspelite found on the beach

Mohawkite, metallic look with white
quartz. Caution, contains arsenic

Prehnite will be pink and/or green,
no "eye" formation

Pudding stone red, black stones
"cemented" together with white quartz.
Note top one has unusual gray color

Quartz typically creamy white

Rhyolite porphyry

Sandstone from U.S. side

Sandstone from Canada near Red Rock

Silver crystal from mine dumps—
very, very rare

Slag from iron smelter

Staurolite "fairy stones" will have
a cross pattern

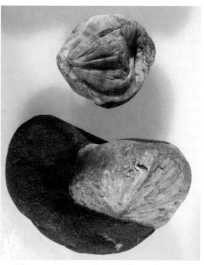

Thomsonite, radiating lines from a
single point, creating an eye effect

Thomsonites loose and in basalt

Thomsonites, Isle Royale,
from a 1960's collection

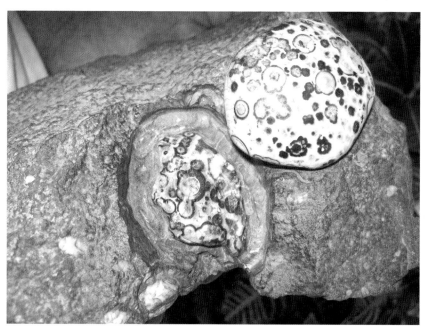

Thomsonites, large rare pieces

Unikite from Batchawana Bay area

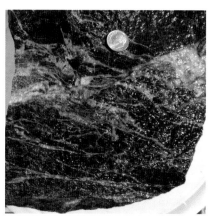

Verde antique marble

Some Types of Lake Superior Agates

Eye agate

Water-leveled agates

Tube agate, note the center stone
is cut horizontal

Sagenite agate

Low-grade agates, agate seams, or partial agates are most commonly found on the lake shore

one agate. It is easy to understand why agates came into existence. It is because of the relative ease with which volcanic ash dissolves. It is not so easy to understand why they are typically banded with alternating red and white bands. There are many theories, no one of them seemingly better than the rest. Vesicular lava weathers rapidly and crumbles, freeing whatever minerals it contains to be scattered by streams, currents, and glaciers.

The best places to look for agates along the lake are the Keweenaw Peninsula and the north shore of the lake in Minnesota and Canada. Points and places where rivers enter the lake and upstream on gravel-filled streams are likely places. The better areas are usually better because they are hard to reach. A Jeep is good to have, or you will need to walk. When you have walked so far that you are ready to give up, you have reached the place where everyone else gave up, and this is the place to start looking. After a heavy storm or in the spring or fall, when not many are on the beaches, is a good time to look.

Lake Superior is no place for amateurs to go boating; storms arise quickly. The water is very cold. Hypothermia sets in quickly. Tall, shear cliffs cut off a retreat to shore in places. Even professionals in big boats get weak-kneed when it storms on this lake.

The lake is not necessarily the best place to look for

agates. During various glacial advances and retreats the eastern outlet of the lake was blocked by ice. When the ice melted during the summer, great floods of water poured out of the west end of the lake and down the St. Croix River to the Mississippi. The town of Moose Lake, Minnesota, about 45 miles south of Duluth, stands on the route these waters, carrying a treasure trove of agates, took. The largest Lake Superior agate on record, 108 pounds, was found here and is on display at the First National Bank. The second largest and others of 15 to 25 pounds were found here. Agates are found wherever there is gravel; along gravel roads, rivers, lakes and in gravel pits. There are three gravel pits open to collectors year round. They even stage an Agate Days Celebration, usually on the second weekend after the 4th of July. Information is available at 1-800-635-3680.

Nearly anywhere there is gravel along the St. Croix and Mississippi rivers you may find agates, with the Prairie du Chien, Wisconsin, and Muscatine, Iowa, gravel pits being well-known hot spots.

"Did I find an agate?"

Translucent, smooth feel with conchoidal fractures. Yes! Yes! You did find an agate!

The number one question asked by those collecting rocks on Lake Superior is... did I find an agate? The name Lake Superior agate implies that you only find this kind of agate on Lake Superior. As we have already mentioned, Lake Superior agates are found in many locations other than Lake Superior. However, it is very exciting and rewarding to find a Lake Superior agate on Lake Superior. These agates are the most sought-after stones when hunting this lake. So it is only fitting to showcase this world famous agate. The most prized Lake Superior agate is the classic red-and-white-banded agate.

The color photo section and the following tips should enable you to answer your own question. It is a matter of eliminating a lot of "want-to-be" agates. In talking to a lot of knowledgeable fellow rock enthusiasts, answering the question, "Do I have an agate?" is like answering how gray must dark gray be before you call it black? Or how much do I alter the white cake recipe before I can call it marble cake? For the purest agate, you will know by the distinctive lines. However, I caution you not to identify agates only by banding. There are many types of agates without banding. I would encourage you to stop at some of the local rock shops to see different collections on site. Take this book....Meanwhile here are some tips to help a novice.

Agates will have all or a combination of the following traits:

Translucent—If you hold the rock in a bright light, the edges of an agate will usually let some light through. Agates are fibrous quartz. Quartz, by nature, is transparent.

Feels greasy or very smooth—The broken surfaces will feel smooth. Amost like running your fingers over a well-polished piece of glass. This is because agates are harder than most other rocks on the beach and will resist scratches, thus a broken surface will remain very smooth.

Conchoidal broken surface—Usually Lake Superior agates will have broken angular chips or dish-like chips. Much like a block of glass that was struck with a hammer a few times, creating conchoidal (shell-like) chips.

Banding—Banding is the most obvious trait when identifying an agate. The banding is usually in a consecutive circular pattern forming almost a bull's eye. But there are dozens of types of Lake Superior agates without consecutive ring banding. See the color section for some other types.

"Potato" shape—Since agates form in gas pockets, a whole agate is usually "potato"-shaped.

Pitted surface—The lining of the gas bubble, which is the outside of the agate, will leave impressions in the stone much like the eyes on a potato.

Colorful—The colors will usually be brighter than other rocks. The most common color is a caramel color, but they also come in a variety of colors including brown, red, white, orange, yellow, peach, and cream.

Tips on looking for agates:
Look in the dry stones for rotten looking potatoes. Most of the stones are one to two inches in diameter. Just before sundown, walk the beach and look for reflections off the rocks. Agates are glassy, and the broken areas will reflect the light.

A thank you to Jeff Anderson, who I consider an expert on agates. He offered many of the tips and identifications above.

Amethyst
Amethyst is quartz with trace amounts of iron or manganese to make the color purple. It is the birthstone of February and is a semi-precious gem. The gem is often faceted into gemstones then set into karat gold. The amethyst on Lake Superior typically is not of gem quality, and it is actually rare to find it on the lake. Many veins of amethyst, which have formed in granite fissuers, are found about 35 miles east of Thunder Bay, Canada, near a town called Pearl. Many veins run north-south and submerge into Lake Superior.

Basalt, amygdaloidal
The gas bubbles in basalt have filled with another mineral.

Basalt, ophitic (textured)
The basalt will look like faint Chinese writing or like a snow flake stuck on the outside. This pattern is all the way through the rock.

Binghamite and Silkstone
Binghamite is from the eastern end of the Cuyuna Iron Ore Range. The color (red) is due to iron oxide. It began as a fibrous goethite now replaced by quartz. The yellow color is due to limonite, also replaced by quartz. Because it, like tigereye, which is really asbestos filled with quartz, is fibrous, it can be cut to produce cat's eye and chatoyant stones.

Silkstone comes in delicate color combinations of yellow, brown, blue, and green. It is another fibrous goethite replacement found in cracks in the shale of Minnesota iron mines in the Cuyuna Range. It, like tigereye, has a chatoyant appearance. Its fibers are seldom straight or parallel to one another. Binghamite sometimes occurs in a flame-like combination with silkstone.

Calcite
Calcite crystals will bubble vigorously with dilute muriatic acid and will scratch easily with a knife. On the

Keweenaw Peninsula they often contain copper sheets and flecks, giving them a red or pink coloration. Some show internal growth stages called phantoms. Some clear calcite with inclusions of copper found here are probably the best found anywhere. Once a year Michigan Technological University holds a Red Metal Retreat with visits to mine sites. Contact the Copper County Rock and Mineral Club of Houghton or the Seaman Mineral Museum at Michigan Tech University. www.museum.mtu.edu, or 906-487-2572.

Chert, Flint, Jasper and Agate

These four minerals are all chemically the same, but have physical differences. Chert, flint, and jasper are all made of granular quartz. They are opaque to light, do not reflect light well, and are dull or waxy in appearance. Chert is light colored and usually comes in nodules. Flint is dark colored and usually comes in layers. Jasper is red in color due to the iron oxide. Agate is fibrous, but not noticeably so. It is noticeably translucent, reflects light well and so has a brighter appearance than the rest.

Unfortunately, these forms of quartz are part of a gradational series that grades from any one to any other, creating a host of in-between wannabes. Chert, flint, jasper, and agate in the Lake Superior area are about 2.1 billion years to about 1 billion years old.

Chert, Flint, Jasper and Hematite

The first three of these minerals occur separately world-wide, but in the Lake Superior basin they, along with hematite, occur together to form a closely related family of minerals. The process that created these minerals in the Lake Superior basin occurred only once, resulting in all of the world's great iron ore deposits. It was a process that can never be repeated. Earth's early atmosphere was made up of methane, ammonia, and water vapor. Iron, in the absence of oxygen, is very soluble. Rain on earth's early iron-rich rocks dissolved iron which remained in solution in earth's early seas. Iron accumulated in sea water for perhaps two and a half billion years. Meanwhile sunlight on the upper atmosphere caused chemical changes to occur, resulting in the production of carbon dioxide through the break down of methane gas and water vapor. Carbon dioxide is what plants utilize as food. Primitive plants similar to blue-green algae evolved. They utilized carbon dioxide and introduced oxygen as a waste product into the sea. Oxygen and iron combined to produce iron oxide (hematite) which settled to the sea floor. Iron oxide is virtually insoluble.

Volcanic ash is filled with easily dissolved minerals which serve as plant fertilizer. In volcanic areas great seasonal blooms of algae occurred, giving rise to a seasonal layer of iron oxide on the sea floor. These primitive plants, like the diatoms and radiolarians of today, seem to have lived in silicon casings. When the bloom faded, their casings rained to the sea floor. The result was a layer of quartz on the sea floor. Each year a layer of hematite and a layer of quartz accumulated on the sea floor. The silicon layer became chert, or if it contained impurities such as carbon from the plants, it became flint. If it contained enough iron oxide, it became jasper. In today's seas, because of the presence of oxygen, this process no longer operates; iron can no longer be stored in solution.

The Lake Superior Basin is what I think of as the jackpot of jasper. Jasper from the iron ore deposits north of the lake is found everywhere on Lake Superior beaches. It is found on waste dumps of the iron mines and in pudding stones, which contain the earliest jasper and iron ore of which I am aware, dating back to 2.4 billion years. Alternating bands of iron ore and jasper can be polished to create extremely attractive stones with built-in contrast. Near Biwabic on the Mesabi Iron Ore Range, about a mile from town, lies the Mary Ellen Mine, whose swirling patterns of jasper and hematite are the standard against which jaspelite, the mixture of jasper and hematite, is measured. In practice, in my experience, nearly any jaspelite is referred to as Mary Ellen Jasper, whether it came from the Mary Ellen Mine or not.

Concretions
These are odd-shaped, wildly exotic growths where

some mineral acting as glue has cemented the clay together. The clay in which these odd shapes occur represents rock ground to powder by the glacier and, therefore, easily dissolved. Calcium carbonate is the glue.

Copper, native

The Keweenaw Peninsula is best known for its native copper contained in vesicles of the local basalt floes and any other openings. One nugget, if you can call it that, weighed 500 tons. Choice specimens are crystallized copper, copper skulls formed around cobbles, and drift copper carried south and freed of stone by the glacier. Copper is collected from mine dumps and is found along the lake. Some of the best collecting occurs when the rock on mine dumps is crushed and spread as gravel on roads. The county garage near its headquarters at Mohawk usually has a pile of crushed rock nearby. Many of the old mining properties are being sold off and access is difficult. Local information is available from Richard Whiteman at Red Metal Minerals. He owns the only operating copper mine. The mine is open for collecting by serious collectors and especially groups. His number is 906-884-6618. Local information is also available from Ken Flood, Keweenaw Gems and Gifts, Inc. His phone number is 906-482-8447. More complete addresses are given on page 99. The book, *Red Gold and Tarnished Silver,* published by the Copper Country Rock and Mineral Club, available from either of these gentlemen, lists 228 collecting sites, and the minerals that may be found at each.

Datolite

Datolite is present as nodules and rarely as crystals in basalt with native copper deposits. It can be found along the lakeshore and in the rock waste near mines on the Keweenaw. Normally it is white, but may be pink, yellow, green, and other colors. Some was scattered to the south by the glacier. As a nodule, usually found in the mine dumps, datolite will look like a head of cauliflower on the outside. During lunch hours, miners used to place bets on these nodules about the inside color, then smash one after another to open. Today it would be like smashing fifty dollar bills at lunch time, depending on the piece. On rare occasions, datolite can be found on the northern shoreline of the Keweenaw. In the colored section of this book, there are examples of two beach datolites.

Diamonds

Many diamonds, some of considerable size, have been found to the south, east and west of Lake Michigan. These were glacial, perhaps from the Lake Superior region, perhaps from farther north where diamonds are being mined on the Arctic coast of Canada. I am not aware of any large diamonds found in the Lake Superior region. Two factors influence how many diamonds will be found in glacial drift: the number of existing diamonds and how many eyes are looking. In the Lake Superior region the population is sparse. It seems probable that the Lake Superior region has as many diamonds as the Lake Michigan region. That doesn't mean you should go and start looking, but if you're there anyway and see something that may be a diamond, check it out.

Kimberlite is a volcanic rock from great depth—some say 400 miles down—that brings diamonds to the surface. Near Lake Ellen in Iron County in Michigan's Upper Peninsula, kimberlite was discovered, but there was less than one carat of diamond to 1000 tons of ore. Nearly two dozen other kimberlitic intrusions have been found in Michigan, but nothing to date of any real interest.

Dolomite, Kona

Kona dolomite, found near Marquette, Michigan, is a well-known cutting material. This is a sedimentary rock laid down on the sea floor by bacteria and algae about two billion two hundred million years ago. The sea was warm and sometimes shallow with gypsum crystals forming. Later the crystals were replaced by unusually pink dolomite. At this time oxygen from plants was just becoming available causing iron, dissolved earlier, to settle out as red iron oxide. When more oxygen was available, the iron ore deposits that surround the lake were laid down. Kona, pink due to its contained iron oxide and black stringers due to carbon from algae, was a hint of what was to come.

The Lindberg Quarry is known for its Kona dolomite. Take U.S. 41 southeast from Marquette to Rt. 480. Go west on 480 to the quarry. There is another quarry near the intersection of routes 41 and 28.

Electrum

Electrum, also called argentium, is a natural gold and silver alloy. Gold ordinarily contains 10 to 15 percent silver. At more than 30 percent silver, it is called electrum. In the unlikely event that you find something that looks like gold, but is too pale yellow to be gold, it may be electrum. It has been found in the Ropes Gold Mining area and other gold mines nearby.

Feldspar

Feldspar is often pink in color, but can be found tan to cream color. It is one of the minerals that make up granite. Feldspar will look like pink quartz when wet on the beach; however, dry, it will have a distinctive reflective plane. The reflection of light from its cleavage plane is best viewed when the stone is dry.

Fulgurites

Fulgurites are grains of sand fused together by lightning to form hollow tubes. Occasionally, they are found at the tops of sand dunes. They range from the size of a pencil to several inches across. The sand must reach a temperature of at least 1710 degrees Celsius to fuse.

Garnet

Garnets are found along the lake in the glacial drift, often in metamorphic rock with much muscovite mica. Nearly all are specimen grade only. Garnets of gem quality can be found in kimberlites, such as the Lake Ellen Kimberlite, but access is unlikely. Garnets can be found in the waste piles of the Beacon Mine on the east side of Beacon, Michigan.

Goethite

Goethite is a common iron ore found in all of the iron mining districts. It occurs in kidney-shaped masses ranging in color from black to yellow brown. Some is banded and can be cut and polished with pleasing results. Some of it, often called limonite, resembles big pieces of rust, which is essentially what it is. It often occurs as stalactites.

Gold

Gold, were it common, would have little value, but because it is uncommon, it has great value. It is, therefore, a foregone conclusion that if you go looking for it, you won't find much. On the Canadian Shield, north of the lake, there are many belts of old metamorphosed basalt. Here gold, silver, copper, zinc, lead, nickel, cobalt, and iron are mined today, along with many other minerals. Carried south by the glacier, drift from these future mining areas was scattered throughout the Lake Superior region.

Because gold is heavier than sand and gravel, it lags behind in streams and is gradually concentrated. Pan in any sand-and-gravel-filled stream entering Lake Superior and you will probably find gold, but not much. Maybe 50 cents worth per hour. This is a project for recreation rather than profit. Sit at home with your kids and watch TV or take them to a movie and it will be another forgotten experience. Take them gold panning and it will be a memorable experience, even if you find nothing at all. Imagine their excitement if you do find even a little gold.

By choosing streams south of places where gold has been mined in the Upper Peninsula, you can improve your odds. There have been many gold mines near Ishpeming, the Ropes Gold Mine near Deer Lake, the mine near Gold Mine Lake, and many others. Gold has been found south of the Gogebic Iron Range.

Gowganda tillite
Gowganda tillite, a metamorphosed glacial till, is from the same area as pudding stone. It is a dark gray stone, usually containing randomly scattered rounded granite pebbles. It is restricted to the east end of the lake. Some of the tillite, or metamorphosed conglomerate, found there is probably nontypical gowganda tillite.

Granite
Since a large portion of Lake Superior's surrounding

bedrock is granite, it is only fitting to say that a majority of the stones on the beaches will be granite. Granites are very colorful when wet or polished. They are used in many commercial purposes such as flooring, countertops, and fireplaces. Granite beach stones will look like speckled rocks. These "specs" are crystals of feldspar, quartz, and biotite (mica). The crystals can develop from flake to dime size. The reds and pinks are from feldspar; the yellow, white, and grays are from quartz; and the black is from biotite.

Greenstone and Greenstone

There is a rock called greenstone, and there is a mineral called greenstone. The rock is metamorphosed basalt. It is mildly green in color, is present on most lake beaches, and is a common stone.

A second type of greenstone is the mineral chlorastrolite, the Michigan state gemstone. These stones are found principally on the Keweenaw Peninsula and Isle Royale, with those from Isle Royale being the best. They have a pattern somewhat like that on a turtle's back or on a Petoskey stone. They are gray-green in color with chatoyant fibers. Most are small stones with the average size being thumbnail size down to pea size. They are amygdaloidal in origin and sometimes intergrow with thompsonites. Those from the Keweenaw tend to be hollow or filled with calcite. Even so, stones of great beauty and considerable value can be cut, just don't cut too deep. Isle Royale is a national park where no collecting is allowed. Chlorasrolite is relatively soft (harness of 5.5-6 on the Mohs scale) when compared to other beach stones. Once a greenstone breaks free from the basalt, the pounding waves will pulverize the stone into sand in about six years.

In the color section there is some Isle Royal greenstone jewelry from a pre-1980s collection.

Half and half
Half and halves are nuggets of native copper with generous inclusions of pure native silver. They can be found rarely along the lake; more commonly in the mine tailings of most copper mines. The Gratiot Mine dumps west of Mohawk and the Osceola Mine dumps at Osceola have yielded many.

Hematite, botrioidal
Specular hematite is iron ore that has been metamorphosed to produce a mass of black, reflective flat flakes ranging in size from tiny to an inch or more across. It looks much like biotite mica, but is much heavier and harder. Mica can be scratched with a fingernail, but hematite cannot. This material, while remarkably attractive as a decorative stone, is not favored by refiners and is considered waste rock. The Champion Mine dumps near the town of Beacon, Michigan, have long been a favorite place to collect. Here a tonnage so vast, that I am unable to even guess at what it might be, has been dumped. There

is some quartz here with some tourmaline and an occasional garnet. The Marquette and Ishpeming Chambers of Commerce have local information.

Mohawkite

Mohawkite was named for the city of Mohawk on the Keweenaw. The term is still favored by rock enthusiasts, but mineralogists prefer the name domeykite and algodonite. It is an attractive compound of arsenic and copper (silver), somewhat resembling pyrite, often embedded in quartz. Its principal source was from mines in the vicinity of Mohawk, Michigan. Tailings rich in Mohawkite were used to build the road to the Kingston Mine. Since this material is largely arsenic, gloves are recommended if cutting and polishing is to be done.

Prehnite

Prehnite, green in color and translucent, can be found in various mine dumps in Keweenaw County such as the Cliff and Phoenix mines. In Ontonagon County it can be found in the Toltec Mine and Minnesota Mine dumps and in lake shore gravels of the Keweenaw Peninsula. The thompsonites found under the soil on Thompsonite Hill overlooking Eagle Harbor are really prehnite with included copper.

Pudding stone

Pudding stone is a very attractive metamorphosed glacial till from 2.4 billion years ago. It consists almost entirely of nothing other than quartz sand, quartz pebbles, jasper, and flint with a little hematite embedded in the jasper. What you have to ask yourself, the first time you see it, is what kind of sorting could produce a rock made of nothing to speak of except one form of quartz or another? It seems probable that the glacier collected its load of quartz from a land surface where prolonged weathering had removed everything other than quartz. In pudding stone are pockets of Kaolinite, a weathering product of feldspar. You also have to ask yourself, if pudding stone is 2.4 billion years old, how old are the pebbles that it is made of? These stones are restricted to the east end of the lake and have come glacially from near Elliot Lake and Bruce and Cobalt in Ontario.

Quartz

Quartz makes up much of the earth's crust. It is found in granites, agates, chert, and is the primary component of sand. Quartz, in a clear mineral form, is usually what gives geodes their sparkle. Light reflects off faces of this six sided crystal giving a sparkle effect. The smaller the crystal, the more faces to reflect light creating more sparkle (druzy quartz). On the beach you will normally find white, off white, or cream quartz. The stone is usually a single color and transparent. Depending on the impurities in the quartz, you can also find yellow, tan, pink, burgundy, green, and gray quartz.

Rhyolite porphyry

Rhyolite porphyry is primarly a red-colored stone with a mix of larger grains of white/gray quartz. These different grain sizes suggest different cooling rates occurred with this stone. It is found throughout the south eastern shoreline.

Sandstone

Sandstone makes up a portion of Lake Superior's bed rock. Beautiful pieces of burgundy and cream-colored sandstone can be found on the lake. On the northern shoreline in Canada, the sand-stone will take on a red and cream color. Sandstone will not take a polish. These rocks are usually picked up because of their unusual spotting. Take a close look, and you will be able to identify this rock easily by the many grains of sand stuck together.

Silver, native

Pure nuggets of silver, some quite large, have rarely been found on the Keweenaw Peninsula. As specimens, they are worth a great deal more than the value of the silver they contain. Most are found in old mine dumps.

Slag

Slag is a man-made first cousin to obsidian. During the last half of the 19th century (1848-1898) charcoal iron was produced, especially in the Upper Peninsula of Michigan, by mixing charcoal with iron ore and setting fire to the charcoal, taking the needed oxygen from the iron ore itself. The same process is still used today in Brazil. Michigan's hardwood forests supplied the wood for charcoal in the UP. To smelt 40 tons of iron per day required the cutting of 7,300 acres of forest per year. Quartz, an impurity in iron ore, melted, became glass, and rose to the surface as slag, a waste product. Charcoal iron was favored for the building of the nation's early railroads, and slag remains as a visual symbol of a chapter in the building of this nation.

Slag, like lava, is full of bubbles, but some is solid enough to cut and polish with pleasing results. It is usually blue, black, green or purple, sometimes with stripes of color. Slag from the smelters was often piled on the ground nearby or dumped into the lake. Near Elk Rapids on Michigan's Lower Peninsula, close to a former smelter near the lake, a cone-shaped hill, flat at the top, has a house at its summit. I am told that the hill is actually a pile of slag.

Former smelters on Michigan's Upper Peninsula were located in Hancock, Houghton, Ontonagon, L'Anse, Iron River, Crystal Falls, Champion, Ishpeming, Negaunee, Palmer, Gwinn, Gladstone, Christmas, Escanaba, St Ignace, Sault Ste. Marie, Newberry, Grand Marais, Manistique, and Fayette (where its smelters and the entire town have been restored), Munising, Marquette, Greenwood, and Clarksburg. Some towns,

like Marquette which had smelters in 7 different locations, had more than one smelter. Just outside Christmas
an old smelter still stands at Christmas Cove. The nearby beach is littered with slag.

Staurolite

Staurolite often comes in pairs, one roughly crossing the
center of the other to form a cross. The cross may be either
a Greek cross (90 degree angle) or more commonly a St.
Andrews cross (60 degree angle). Look on the south side of
Lake Michigamme about a mile and a half south of
Michigamme, Michigan, in the road cuts and the
surrounding area. These crossed crystal pairs are often
called fairy crosses. Crystals are usually stubby and small,
the size of the end of your thumb or smaller, often altered
at the surface by weathering. Staurolite is a metamorphic
mineral.

Thomsonites

Thomsonites, like Lake Superior agates, form in the vesicles
of basalt and rhyolite lavas. The Minnesota thomsonites are
sought even more avidly than Lake Superior agates and are
considered the best there are. The best of the Minnesota
thomsonites are found along the lake with the Terrace Point
basalt floe being the major source. Good Harbor Bay, just
southwest of Grand Marais, is a good place to look.
Thomsonite Beach near Good Harbor Bay is the best place
to look, but is only open to guests of the Thomsonite Beach

Inn. In addition to loose thomsonites on the beaches and in the soil, the 160 foot thick Terrace Point basaltic lava floe contains thomsonites not yet released by weathering.

On Thomsonite Hill overlooking Copper Harbor, prehnite with a strong resemblance to thomsonite, can be found under the soil.

Unikite

Unikite is orange or pinkish granite with light green streaks of epidote. Because there is no granite on the south side of the lake, unikite found there is glacial from the north, from the Pancake Bay area. Unikite is found along the south shore of the lake from its eastern end to at least as far west as the Two Hearted River. Some found here is as attractive as any found anywhere. Some has been considered good enough for mounting in gold jewelry.

Verde antique

The Verde Antique Quarry is a few hundred feet from the Ropes Gold Mine near Ishpeming, Michigan. Verde antique, which means old green, is serpentine with included calcite and dolomite. This is the type of material that might be best used for bookends, doorstops and other large-stone decorative items.

Fossils

Lake Superior, especially its west end, was free of ice for several hundred years before the axe of extinction fell for mastodons, mammoths, and giant beavers the size of a black bear. Many of their skeletons have been found farther south, but none, so far as I know, in the Lake Superior Basin. Mammoths and mastodons in particular would walk out onto thin ice above a marsh or pond, break through and sink into the muck. Such remains are usually found while digging for construction projects. Because there are so few people in the Lake Superior region, and thus very little digging, the remains of these animals, along with the antlers of reindeer and horns of musk ox, have not been found to prove that these animals once roamed Lake Superior's shores. Should you see a very large bone or a horn projecting from a bank of sand, gravel or clay, check it out.

When the Great Lakes were brim full of water, about 4000 years ago, whales were able to swim into the Great Lakes. The remains of these intelligent and apparently curious creatures, bowhead, fin, and sperm, have been found on earlier higher beaches on Michigan's Lower Peninsula. None has been found on Lake Superior's early beaches. The whales may have come in by way of the Mississippi River, the Mohawk Hudson, or the St. Lawrence. There is no apparent reason why they would not have entered Lake Superior. If you find fossils such as these, it is by sheer blind luck.

A sign erected by park service personnel at the Pictured Rocks states that "any fossils found on these shores have come from Hudson Bay." A region to the southwest of Hudson Bay, the Hudson Bay Lowland which extends out into Hudson Bay, is floored by up to 6000 feet of Ordovician, Silurian and Devonian rock, as well as Cretaceous sediments. Not many, but some, of these fossils were scattered along Lake Superior's shores by way of the glacier.

There are fossils in the Cambrian sandstones that line the southern lake shore, but they are uncommon, poorly preserved and do not stand up to wave action for any length of time. Any other fossils found along the lake or in the mines that surround the lake are Pre-Cambrian in age, and Pre-Cambrian fossils are generally microscopic in size with two exceptions. In Kona dolomite many wavy line-like laminations caused by algae growing on the sea floor can be seen. Similar laminations can be seen in some iron formations. These are called stromatoperoids.

In the Negaunee iron formation near Negaunee, Michigan

a scientist by the name of Tau-Ming Han found the oldest Pre-Cambrian macrofossils (large) known. These are fossil-coiled filaments up to two feet long representing algae capable of utilizing sunlight. Unfortunately, these are barely visible on the bedding planes where they occur. When they do contrast well with the stone, they are very nice, and because of their age, two point one billion years old, of great interest. Many types of blue-green algae and bacteria can be seen under the microscope, in thin sections of the gunflint chert and in iron formations, but here you are dealing with micro-fossils measured in microns. These are also of great interest, but not to the average collector.

Mining in the Keewenaw Peninsula, Michigan

The Keewenaw Peninsula is the fingerlike peninsula that juts out into Lake superior from Michigan's Upper Peninsula. This area is extremely rich in minerals including copper, silver, greenstone, datolite, thompsonite, prehnite, and many others. It is the only place in the world where pure copper formed in such large masses. Copper mining operations elsewhere pulverize the rock then extract trace amounts of copper by smelting or by chemical or electrolitic methods.

Mining native copper in Keweenaw has a long and rich history. Local Native Americans came to the area using crude stone tools to mine small copper outcrops for mak-

ing copper tools. Many of the earliest copper tools origi-
nated from a surface outcrop of copper in the Keweenaw
Peninsula. As more uses of copper came into play, the
demand for copper increased. This led European investors
to the region and the commercialization of the copper mining began.

It started in 1766 when a fur trapper named Alexander
Henry discovered a 6,500 pound piece of float copper lying
on an Ontonagon riverbank. By 1771-1772 a mining company from London made the first real mining attempts in
the area. The Victoria Dam, near Victoria, Michigan, now
covers the site where these failed attempts were made. By
the mid-1800s numerous mines began operating in the
region. Fissures with massive veins of pure copper produced some very profitable mines. The Cliff Mine, opened
in 1845 and closed in 1870, paid out dividends of more
than 2.6 million dollars! The Minnesota Mine opened in
1848 and operated for only 22 years, but paid out 1.8 million dollars in dividends. The Central Mine's original
investment of $100,000.00 paid out 1.9 million dollars
during its operation. At the mining peak, there were 21
stamping mills with a capacity of stamping 59,400 tons of
copper per day. At full capacity, with today's copper prices,
the production in the Keweenaw area would equate to
356.4 million dollars per day! That's 14.8 million an hour!
It goes to show you how significant copper mining was in
the Copper County. (These figures do not include other

large mining operations in areas such as those near WaWa, Canada, and Michipicoten Island.) It also goes to say that some investors lost lots of money on copper veins that pinched out and were short lived. By the early 1930s, copper was selling for five cents per pound, and much of the mining operations were discontinued.

Mine Dumps

In the Lake Superior Basin there have been two principal types of mining operations carried out; copper and iron mining. Because of financial considerations, mining has always resembled an enterprise that in appearance might well have been designed by Neanderthal cave men. Blast down the rock with explosives, truck the best of the ore to the first of a series of machines that will, at the end of the series, spit out the desired product; in this case iron or copper. Anything other than the best of the ore is a costly distraction to be disposed of on the mine dump as rapidly and as cheaply as possible. As a result, much that is of interest to collectors ends up on the waste heap. Agates, datolite, chlorasrolites, garnets, staurolite, copper, silver, jasper and a long list of other minerals wind up on the dump, which makes the dump a collector's paradise. There is more waste on the mine dumps in the Lake Superior Basin than one man could go through with a pick and shovel in a million years.

Access to mine dumps is not easy. Permission must be obtained, and because much of the land is currently changing hands, permission is not always easy to obtain. The surfaces of the dumps have been gone over pretty well. The material on the dumps is often quite coarse, making digging difficult, and some of the mine dumps are grown over with weeds, grass, and even trees. However, the dumps are mined for crushable rock by private contractors for road gravel, as well as by county road crews. Dumps that have been recently mined for fresh gravel are prime places to look. They are also bulldozed for various mineral-collecting events arranged by local rock clubs and chambers of commerce. Gravel roads freshly covered in new gravel are good places to look, particularly for copper and related minerals.

For native copper a metal detector is useful. I know of one gentleman who attached a metal detector to an A.T.V. and drove over the glacial debris to the south of the Keweenaw. He is said to have collected 15 to 30 thousand dollars worth of copper per year. With diligence, planning, and effort you should be able to come away from a mine-dump-collecting trip with anything from a pick-up truck load of common stuff, like specular hematite or jaspelite, to a fair number of specimens of less common but extremely desirable minerals.

Iron Mine Dumps

Iron is the fourth most abundant element in the earth's crust, with oxygen being the most abundant, and silicon being the second most abundant. Oxygen and silicon combine to produce the quartz, chert, flint and jasper found with iron ore.

Iron combines with oxygen to produce minerals of red, brown, and yellow colors. The minerals most commonly found on iron mine dumps are hematite, magnetite, goethite (also called limonite), pyrite, jasper, chert, jaspelite, garnets, tourmaline, quartz, specular hematite, botrioidal hematite, staurolite, and very rarely beryl and topaz. Not all of these will be found on any one dump.

Copper Mine Dumps

The minerals most commonly found on copper mine dumps are copper, datolite, chlorastrolite, prehnite, copper and silver mix, native silver (not common), calcite with included copper, quartz crystals, Mohawkite, chrysocolla, copper skulls, copper crystals, silver crystals, hematite crystals and agates. Not all of these are to be found on any one mine dump.

Safety

Mining areas are much more dangerous than the lakeshore. Stay away from mine machinery; it's not only dangerous, it's expensive, and mine owners don't want anyone near it. Stay away from quarry edges and at the bottom of a quarry stay away from loose rock above. Watch out for an unfilled mine shaft lurking open behind some bush; some go straight down far enough to give you time to think over at least some of your sins before you hit bottom. One of the mines on the Keweenaw is nearly two miles deep. Stay out of horizontal mine shafts; some have holes in the floor that go down to a lower level. There may be loose rock on the ceiling. The only man ever killed by a dinosaur was killed by a loose stone cast of a dinosaur footprint that fell out of the ceiling as the man was walking underneath.

Copper Cleaning

The recipe for cleaning tarnished native copper to get that bright, clean, red coppery look was furnished by Keweenaw Gem and Gift, Inc., which was kind enough to allow us to publish it.

Unless you have a great deal of copper to clean or are just naturally an obsessive-compulsive type, it makes no sense financially or otherwise to purchase and assemble all of the chemicals and equipment you will need to do the job. Muriatic acid, which is simply a less than laboratory pure form of hydrochloric acid, can be purchased at almost any hardware store. It is inexpensive. Nitric acid, on the other hand, is difficult to get, expensive, troublesome to ship from whatever source you can locate, if indeed you can locate a source, and it is dangerous to use.

Both Keweenaw Gem and Gift and Red Metal Minerals will clean copper for you for what I consider to be a nominal price. They have the benefit of years of experience and will almost certainly do a better, cleaner, less expensive job than you can do yourself. Addresses and phone numbers for Keweenaw Gem and Gifts and Red Metal Minerals are given on page 101.

Should you wish to do it yourself, the procedure is as follows:

1. Remove unwanted rock by picking, hammering at specimens to be cleaned. Wire brush rock to remove loose, soft material. Wash with high pressure water gun, if possible.

2. Soak in muriatic acid (hydrochloric) approximately 1 hour. Sometimes toilet bowl cleaners contain this acid. This soaking removes all the green/brown oxidation from copper, plus any calcite is dissolved. If lots of green oxidation is present, use a longer acid dip.

3. Rinse well and brush the copper and rock again to remove any further loose rock. Wash with high-pressure water.

4. Dip in diluted nitric acid (30 seconds to 1 minute MAXIMUM). This is a very strong acid, so be prepared. Wear goggles, rubber gloves, and use only in a well-ventilated area—OUTDOORS ONLY!! Keep running water nearby to rinse spills and splashes on the ground or clothing. Rinse the copper many times until no acid remains on or in the copper specimen (15-30 minutes). Rinse one last time with hot water prior to using Copper Brite dip.

UNDER NO CIRCUMSTANCES SHOULD ACID BE ALLOWED TO REACT WHERE IT FOAMS AND BUBBLES, CAUSING VERY POISONOUS REDDISH FUMES.

DILUTE AND RINSE AT ONCE!

5.   Dip copper into solution of Copper Brite. Any liquid brass/copper cleaner may work.
1 vial Copper Brite = 1 gal mix (reusable)
     RINSE, RINSE, RINSE (1-2 hours if needed).

Rinse until no yellowish coloration remains in the rinse water. Towel dry, dry with a hair dryer, or dry with a fan.

6.   Spray with clear acrylic laquer one day after the copper has been cleaned and dried. If the copper tarnishes, redo the process. Weak acids and/or not enough rinsing are the primary problems causing tarnishing.

   Note: Muriatic Acid to Copper Brite = look of satin finish.
          Muriatic Acid to Nitric to Copper Brite = look of a glossy finish.

Precautions
- Always wear goggles, rubber gloves, and an apron.
- Keep running water close by to dilute and rinse spills.
- Use plastic pails/containers for holding the acids. Cover well when not in use.
- Make sure all the acids/solutions are labeled correctly.
- All acid work must be done outdoors away from children, animals, plants, cars, houses, etc.
- Clean water is the best rinse. We do not recommend ammonia, caustic soda, or any other neutralizer.

Rock Shops

The following is a list of rock shop owners and others willing and able to be helpful.

Ernest Johnson
906-228-9422
1962 West Fair
Marquette, MI 49855

John Heikkinen
Nature's Picks Rock Shop
600 E. Cloverland Dr.
Ironwood, MI 49938
906-932-7340

Prospectors Paradise
Alex & Darlene Fagotti
P. O. Box 86
Mohawk, MI 49950
906-337-6889

Agate City
Bob & Nancy Lynch
eMail: agatecity@frontiernet.net
Two Harbors, MN 55616
218-834-2304

Copper Country Collectibles
www.coppercountrycollectibles.com
Randy & Lisa Bicigo
P. O. Box 214
Mohawk, MI 49950
877-337-2474

The New Keweenaw Agate Shop
Les Tolonen
U. S. 41 - P. O. Box 20
Copper Harbor, MI 49918

Keweenaw Gem & Gift, Inc.
1007 W. Memorial
Houghton, MI 49931
906-482-8447 or (800) 554-8447
email: copper@up.net
Ken Flood

Red Metal Minerals
Richard Whiteman
906-884-6618
email: redmetals@charter.net

The A. E. Seaman Mineral Museum
Michigan Technological University
Houghton, MI 49931
906-487-2572

Beaver Bay Agate Shop & Museum
Keith & Teresa Bartel
P. O. Box 395, 1003 Main St.
Beaver Bay, MN 55601-0395

Cliffs Shaft Mine Museum
Marquette Range Iron Mining
Heritage Theme Park, Inc.
P.O. Box 555
Ishpeming, MI 49849
906-485-1882

Mine Tours

Tom Poynter & Lani Hendricks-Poynter
Delaware Mine
7804 Delaware Mine Rd.
Mohawk, MI 49950
906-289-4688

Adventure Mine
Greenland, MI
12 miles east of Ontonagon off M-38
www.adventuremine.com
906-883-3371

Quincy Mine
Hancock, MI
906-482-3101

Maps

DeLorme Maps of Wisconsin
ISBN 0-89933-331-1

DeLorme Maps of Minnesota
ISBN 0-89933-333-8

DeLorme Maps of Michigan
ISBN 0-89933-335-4

The Lake Superior Maps
888-244-5253

The Only Complete Map of Lake Superior
11 x 17 laminated ISBN 0-942235-52-2
24 x 36 Plain ISBN 0-942235-46-0
24 x 36 Laminated ISBN 0-942235-47-9